www.raintreepublishers.co.uk
Visit our website to find out more information about Raintree books.

To order:
Phone 0845 6044371
Fax +44 (0) 1865 312263
Email myorders@raintreepublishers.co.uk

Customers from outside the UK please telephone +44 1865 312262

Raintree is an imprint of Capstone Global Library Limited, a company incorporated in England and Wales having its registered office at 7 Pilgrim Street, London, EC4V 6LB – Registered company number: 6695582

First published in hardback in 2012
First published in paperback in 2013

Edited by Daniel Nunn, Rebecca Rissman, and Harriet Milles
Designed by Ryan Frieson
Picture research by Tracy Cummins
Originated by Capstone Global Library Ltd.
Production by Victoria Fitzgerald
Printed and bound in China by Leo Paper Products Ltd

ISBN 978 1 406 22904 2 (hardback)
15 14 13 12 11
10 9 8 7 6 5 4 3 2 1

ISBN 978 1 406 22971 4 (paperback)
16 15
10 9 8 7 6 5 4 3

British Library Cataloguing in Publication Data
Rissman, Rebecca.
What is a family?. – (Acorn plus)
1. Families–Pictorial works–Juvenile literature.
I. Title II. Series
306.8′5-dc22
A full catalogue record for this book is available from the British Library.

Acknowledgements
We would like to thank the following for permission to reproduce photographs: Corbis **p. 11** (© David P. Hall); Getty Images **pp. 7** (Tim Hall), **15 right** (Stephen Simpson), **19** (© Radius Images); istockphoto **pp. 5 left** (© RonTech2000), **6** (© Catherine Yeulet), **8** (© Silvia Jansen), **9** (© Joseph C. Justice Jr.), **10** (© paul kline),**12** (© James Pauls),**13** (© Juhász Péter), **14** (© Agnieszka Kirinicjanow), **16** (© Carmen Martínez Banús); Shutterstock **pp. 4** (© Paul Prescott), **5 right**, **18** (© iofoto), **15 left** (© BlueOrange Studio), **17**, **20** (© cabania), **21** (© bikeriderlondon).

Front cover photograph of a family group reproduced with permission of Getty Images (Anthony Plummer). Back cover photographs reproduced with permission of istockphoto (© Catherine Yeulet).

We would like to thank Anne Pezalla for her invaluable help in the preparation of this book.

Families

What is Family?

Rebecca Rissman

Contents

Some words appear in bold, **like this**. You can find out what they mean in "Words to know" on page 23.

What is a family?

A family is a group of people who care for each other. Families can be very different.

Some families are large. They have many **family members**. Other families are very small. They have few family members.

Some people in families are **related**. This means they come from the same parent, grandparent, or great grandparent. People can be related in many ways.

Some people in families are not related. People who are **married** are not related to each other. Children who are **adopted** are not related to their parents.

Siblings

Some families include **siblings**. Siblings are children from the same parents. Brothers are male siblings. Sisters are female siblings. Step-siblings are children from different parents.

Siblings can be older or younger than you. Siblings can look alike, or different. And siblings can even be **twins**. Twins are siblings who were born at the same time from the same parents.

Parents

Some families include parents. Parents are adults who care for children. Male parents are called fathers. Sometimes they are called dads. Female parents are called mothers. Sometimes they are called mums.

Some parents are **divorced**. Divorced parents live apart but still care for their children. Some divorced parents **re-marry**. The person that a divorced parent marries becomes your **step-parent**.

Aunts and uncles

Some families include aunts or uncles. The **siblings** of your parents are your aunts and uncles. Female siblings of a parent are called aunts. Male siblings of a parent are called uncles.

Sometimes special family friends are called aunt or uncle. They are close friends who are not **related** to the family.

Cousins

Some families include cousins. Your cousins are the children of your aunts and uncles.

Some families include many cousins. Some families include few cousins. Some families don't have any cousins at all.

Grandparents

Some families include grandparents. Grandparents are your parents' parents. Grandparents who are women are called grandmothers. Grandparents who are men are called grandfathers.

Some grandparents live with their families. Sometimes younger **family members** might help to take care of their grandparents.

Foster parents

Foster parents are adults who care for children they are not **related** to. Foster parents help keep children safe.

Some foster parents care for the same child for a long time. Some foster parents care for a child for a short time.

Role models

Role models are special people who help others be their best. Role models are people who set good examples for others. Role models can help you to learn things, too.

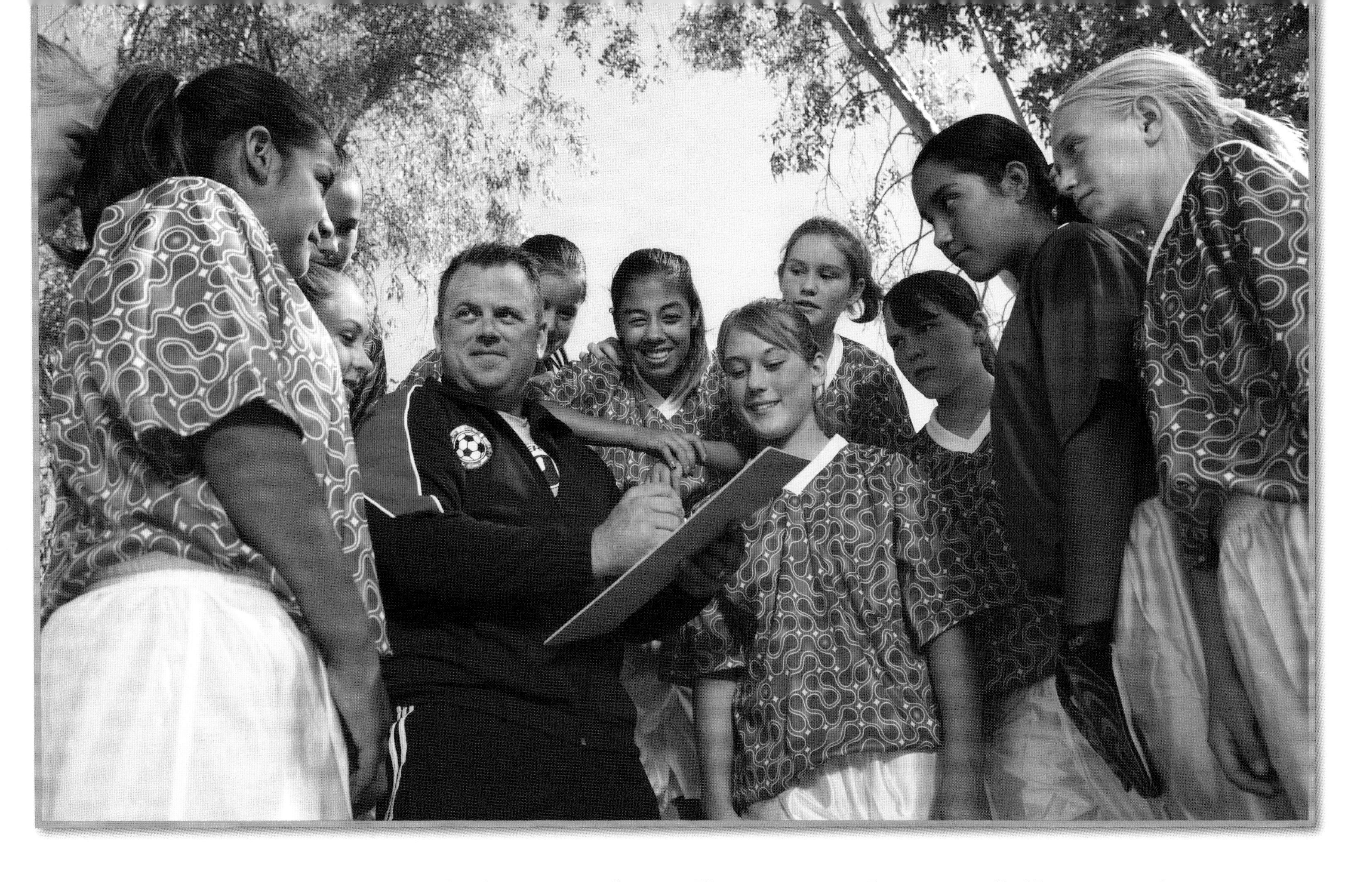

Some role models are **family members.** Other role models are special friends who are leaders. Some role models are people you've never even met!

Family tree

Grandfather
Grandmother
Father
Mother
Uncle
Aunt
Uncle
Sister
You
Brother
Cousin
Cousin

Words to know

adopted welcomed into a new family. Many families adopt children.

divorced no longer married

family member person belonging to a family

married when two people are bonded by law. When two people love each other, they may decide to get married.

related coming from the same family members. Children born from the same mother or father are related.

re-marry when adults marry again. Some parents remarry after a divorce.

sibling brother or sister

step-parent person a divorced parent marries

twins two siblings born at the same time from the same mother and father

Index

Notes for parents and teachers

Before reading

Show the children the front cover of the book. Guide children in a discussion about what they know about families. Tell children that all families are different.

After reading

- Tell the children they are going to write about their families. Ask each child to describe the people in their family. Then ask them to write one thing that is special about their family. Afterwards, ask them to draw a picture of their family and label their family members.